Mothers & Daughters

PLACE PHOTO HERE! PLACE PHOTO HERE! PLACE PHOTO HERE! PLACE PHOTO HERE! PLACE PHOTO HERE! PLACE PHOTO HERE!

A Record Book About us

Mothers & Daughters

A Record Book for

Annalee & Laura

Contents

Contents

What a Pair!

A photo of the two of us

Mother

Daughter

Day I was born 12-1?-19 67

Where I was born SELLERSVILLE, PA

Where I grew up RED HILL, PA

Day I was born 01-11-2001

Where I live now CREAMERY PA

Where I was born Doylestown, PA

Where I grew up 1100 CRESSMA RD Creamery

Where I live now

Mother

&

Daughter

Similarities in personality

Personality differences

The features we share

Curly Hair

2nd & Third Toes Joining (Ruth family)

Dimples

Unique features of our own

Annalee → Hazel eyes, freckles

Beauty Mark above lip - mom

Lefty - mom

I See You in Me...

first saw myself in you when...

_____

_____

_____

_____

_____

_____

Phrases and sayings we share

_____

_____

_____

Things we do alike

_____

_____

_____

Free to Be You & Me

The unique things about us

You are special because

We both like... chocolate, Tomatoes, Reading, lavender

Dogs,

We disagree on liking...

Photograph

The Many Roles a Woman Plays

Mother
Daughter
Friend
Partner
Wife
Colleague

Mother
Daughter
Friend
Partner
Wife
Colleague

The roles I enjoy most _____

_____

_____

_____

_____

The roles you enjoy most _____

_____

_____

_____

_____

Family Life

Important Family Times Together

_____

_____

_____

_____

_____

_____

_____

_____

We always... GO TO DELAWARE WATER GAP ON LABOR DAY

Photo

Name

Name

Photo

Photo

The Fam

Name

Name

Name

Photo

Photo

A Place of My Own

My Home

My favorite things about my house
_____
_____
_____
_____

Here is a description of my favorite room
_____
_____
_____

Lingering projects...
_____
_____
_____

Photo

A Place of Your Own

Your Home

Your favorite things about your home
_____
_____
_____
_____

What makes your home uniquely yours
_____
_____
_____
_____

Photo

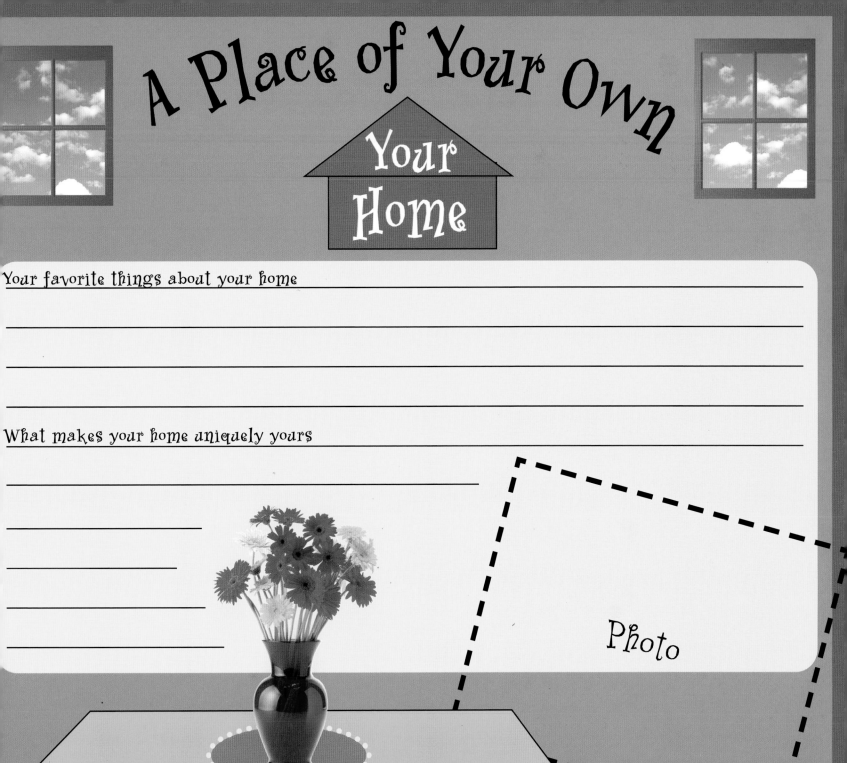

Reaching for the Stars!

I was so proud of you when...

You were so proud of me when...

Award Certificate

This award is presented to

for

signed

The Men In Our Lives

My favorite thing about my father

Your favorite thing about your father

PHOTO

PHOTO

Good tips you've taught me about men

Qualities I admire in men

Lots of Love!

Photo

Photo

The things we love most about each other

Love advice

_____

_____

_____

_____

_____

_____

_____

_____

_____

_____

_____

_____

_____

Best lesson you've taught me about love

_____

_____

_____

_____

_____

_____

Not Just Family, But Friends

Our friendship makes me happy because...

Things I love to share with you

The time we spend together is special because...

Photo

Photo

Photo

Photo

The Days in Which We Grew Up

What I love most about my generation

_____

_____

_____

_____

Things that keep me youthful

_____

_____

_____

What I admire about your generation

_____

_____

_____

Things that get better as I get older

What I admire about your generation

Things that are important to me now

The Days in Which We Grew Up

Listen to Your Mother!

I guess it's safe to tell you now...

Lessons learned the hard way

Can you believe the time this happened...

Crackin' Up

We always laughed about...

Remember the time...

Funniest jokes & stories we share _____

_____

_____

_____

_____

_____

_____

_____

Humor has been good for us because

_____

_____

_____

_____

_____

_____

_____

Photograph

Photograph

Time for Each Other

Things we enjoy doing indoors

Things we enjoy doing outdoors

Favorite places to eat out

_____

_____

_____

_____

_____

_____

_____

_____

Best places to go shopping

_____

_____

_____

_____

_____

_____

_____

_____

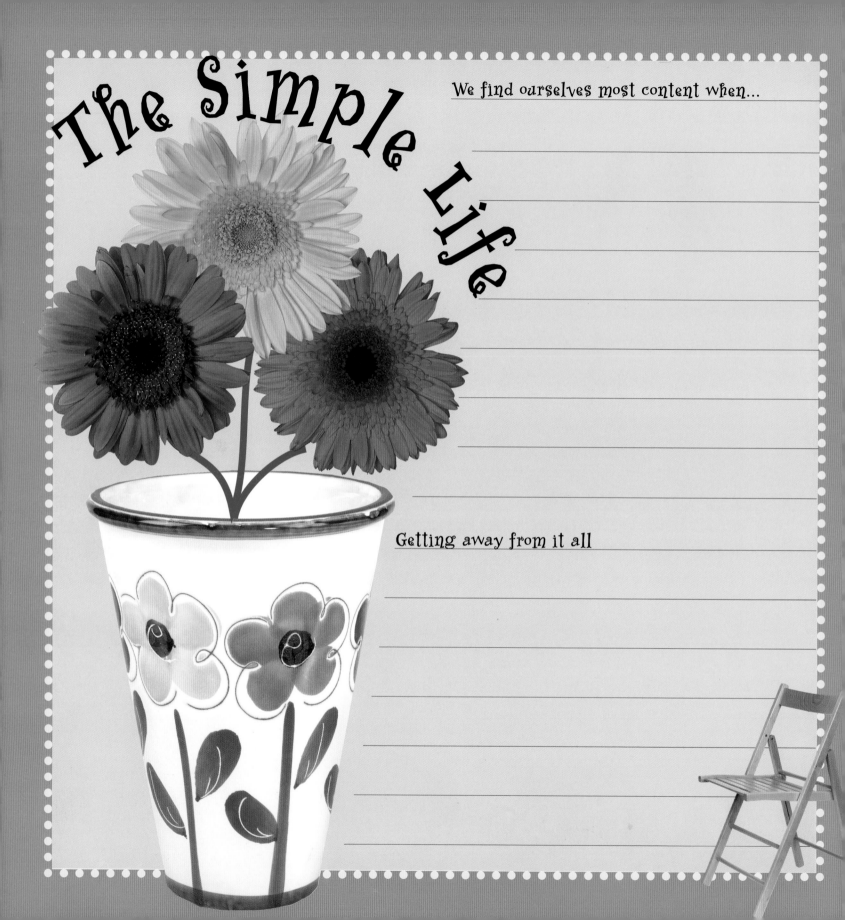

The Simple Life

We find ourselves most content when...

_____

_____

_____

_____

_____

_____

_____

Getting away from it all

_____

_____

_____

_____

_____

_____

_____

Little things that
make us happy

In our free time we like to

We like to keep fit by

Dieting dilemmas

Body
&
Mind

Strengthening our minds

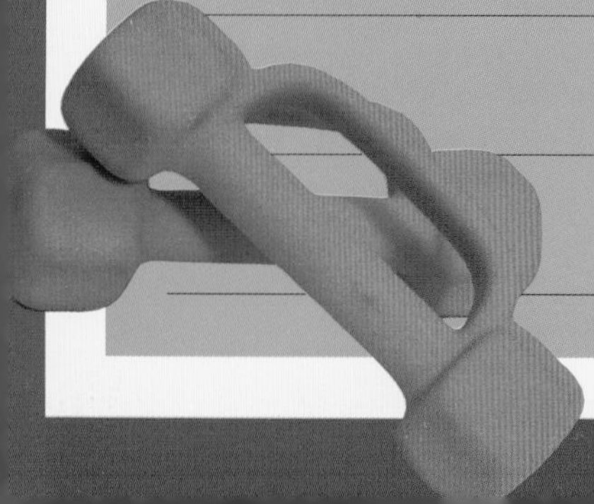

Pampering

Fitness & inner beauty tips

Photographs

Photographs

HEADLINES

Talking Politics

Important World Events of Today

Important Social Issues

A Different World

Spring

Our favorite things about Summer

Summer

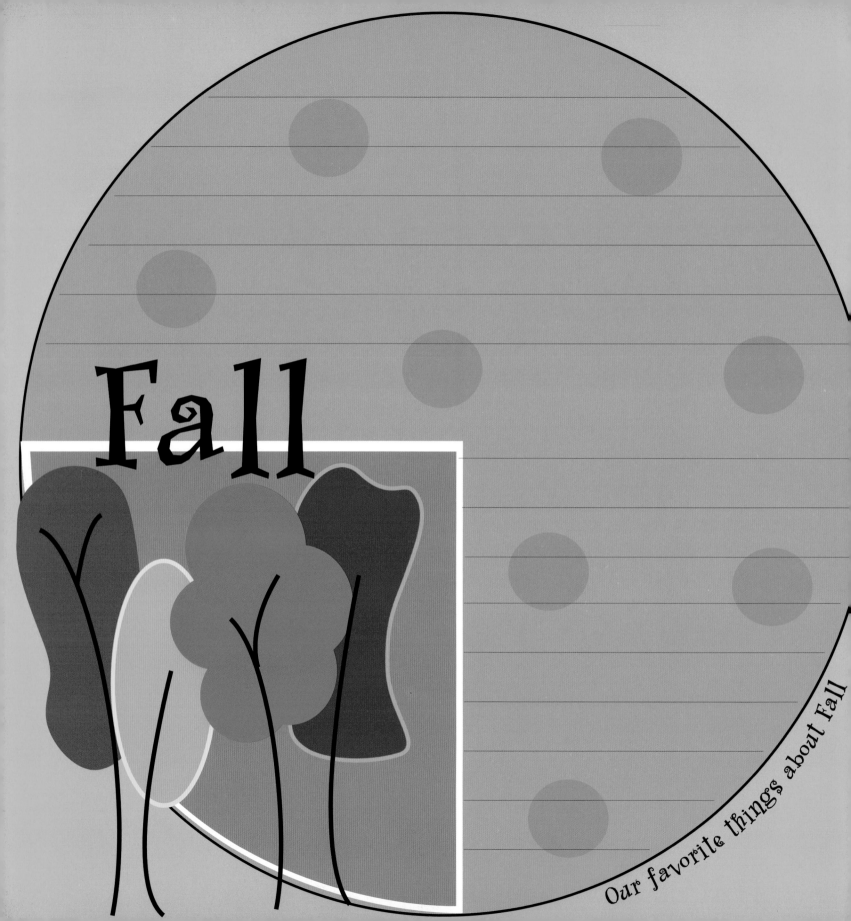

Fall

Our favorite things about Fall

Winter

PHOTO

PHOTO

Fun
in the
Sun

Photo

We like to fill our day by...

Moonlight Magic

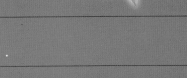

At night it's fun to...

Photo

Advice you've given me about cooking

Most disastrous kitchen moment

In the Kitchen

Our favorite dishes

_____
_____
_____
_____
_____
_____

Recipes you've handed down

_____
_____
_____
_____
_____

Photograph

Photograph

Favorite traveling experience

_____
_____
_____
_____
_____
_____
_____
_____
_____
_____
_____
_____
_____

Traveling

The most exciting place
we traveled together to
_____
_____
_____
_____
_____
_____
_____
_____
_____
_____
_____
_____

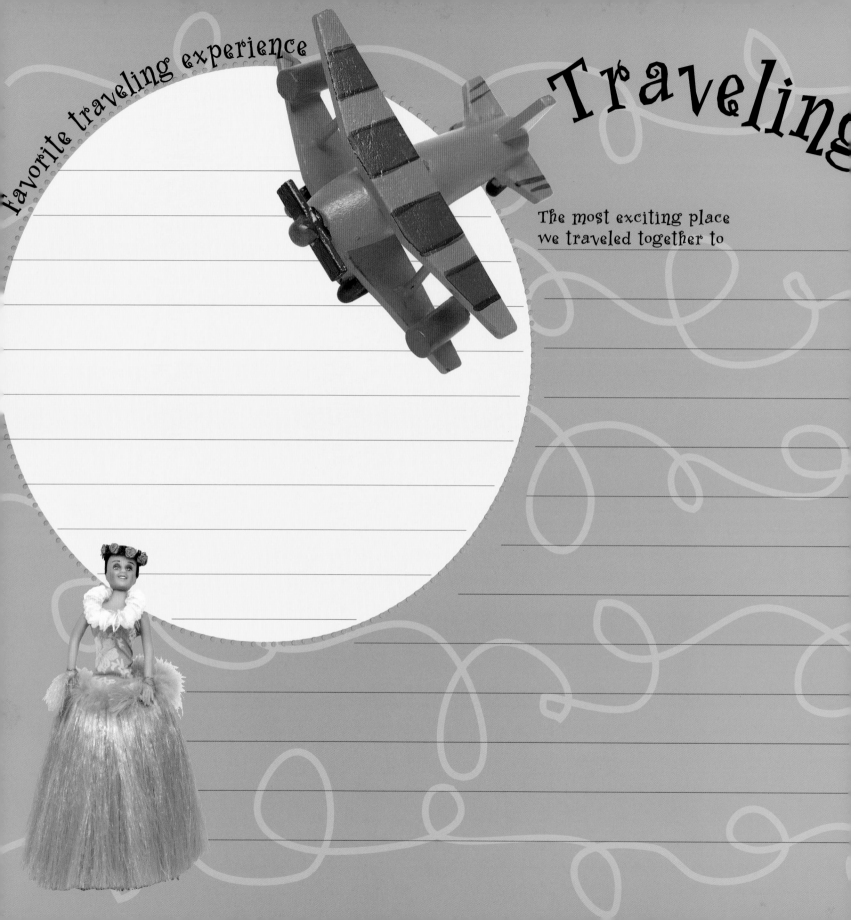

Adventures Together

orite places to stay
_____
_____
_____
_____
_____
_____

the road...
_____
_____
_____
_____

Most bizarre place we've been
_____
_____
_____

Moments we'd like to forget
_____
_____
_____
_____
_____

Role Models

Women that inspire me
_____
_____
_____
_____
_____
_____
_____

I would love to meet...
_____
_____
_____

Qualities I most admire in people
_____
_____
_____

Influential people in my life
_____
_____
_____
_____

_____
_____
_____
_____

What I Wish for You

What You Wish for Me

Other Available Record Books From Havoc!

A Celebration
of Memories

A Circle of Love

A Cool Couple

Baby

College Life

Couples

Our Family

Forever Friends

Friendship

Generations

Girlfriends

Grandmother

Grandparents

Heart to Heart

It's All About Me!

Mothers & Daughters

Mother & Son

My Pregnancy

Our Honeymoon

Our Wedding

School Days

Sisters

Memories of My Garden

Tying the Knot

Twins

Your First Five Years

havoc

PUBLISHING